**STOP GETTING IN
YOUR OWN WAY**

CLEAR YOUR PATH

Do Whatever It Takes to Move
Forward With Grace

Joy Burns

Table of Contents

Chapter 1: Why You Are Amazing 6
Chapter 2: Just Try 9
Chapter 3: The Magic of the 5 Minute Rule 13
Chapter 4: Meditation The Key To Happiness 16
Chapter 5: How to Learn Faster 19
Chapter 6: Don't Fear Judgement 22
Chapter 7: 10 Habits of Meryl Streep 25
Chapter 8: The Things That Matter 29
Chapter 9: *Stop Ignoring Your Health* 34
Chapter 10: How To Not Live Your Life In Regret 36
Chapter 11: Blaming Others In Your Life For Your Mistakes 43
Chapter 12: How to Love Yourself First 45
Chapter 13: **Start Working On Your Dreams Today** 48
Chapter 14: How To Take Action 52
Chapter 15: Live Life To The Fullest 56
Chapter 16: Removing The Things In Your Day That Don't Serve A Purpose for You 58
Chapter 17: *How To Achieve Peak Performance In Your Career* 60
Chapter 18: 6 Ways To Define What Is Important In Your Life 64
Chapter 19: Five Habits For An Extremely Productive Day 68
Chapter 20: How Your Beliefs And Moods Contribute To What's Going On In Your Life 71
Chapter 21: Making Sky The Limit 74
Chapter 22: Five Habits of A Healthy Lifestyle 77
Chapter 23: Bounce Back From Failure 81
Chapter 24: How to Value Being Alone 84
Chapter 25: Happy People Stay Present 87
Chapter 26: 5 Lessons on Being Wrong 89

Chapter 27: How To live Your Best Life 91
Chapter 28: How To Set Smart Goals 94
Chapter 29: 10 Habits of Mariah Carey 97
Chapter 30: 10 Habits of Jennifer Lawrence 101
Chapter 31: 10 Habits of Kamala Harris 105
Chapter 32: 10 Habits of Lady Gaga 109

Chapter 1:
Why You Are Amazing

When was the last time you told yourself that you were amazing? Was it last week, last month, last year, or maybe not even once in your life?

As humans, we always seek to gain validation from our peers. We wait to see if something that we did recently warranted praise or commendation. Either from our colleagues, our bosses, our friends, or even our families. And when we don't receive those words that we expect them to, we think that we are unworthy, or that our work just wasn't good enough. That we are lousy and under serving of praise.

With social media and the power of the internet, these feelings have been amplified. For those of us that look at the likes on our Instagram posts or stories, or the number of followers on Tiktok, Facebook, or Snapchat, we allow ourselves to be subjected to the validation of external forces in order to qualify our self-worth. Whether these are strangers who don't know you at all, or whoever they might be, their approval seems to matter the most to us rather than the approval we can choose to give ourselves.

We believe that we always have to up our game in order to seek happiness. Everytime we don't get the likes, we let it affect our mood for the rest of the day or even the week.

Have you ever thought of how wonderful it is if you are your best cheerleader in life? If the only validation you needed to seek was from yourself? That you were proud of the work you put out there, even if the world disagrees, because you know that you have put your heart and soul into the project and that there was nothing else you could have done better in that moment when you were producing that thing?

I am here to tell you that you are amazing because only you have the power to choose to love yourself unconditionally. You have the power to tell yourself that you are amazing. and that you have the power to look into yourself and be proud of how far you came in life. To be amazed by the things that you have done up until this point, things that other people might not have seen, acknowledged, or given credit to you for. But you can give that credit to yourself. To pat yourself on the back and say "I did a great job".

I believe that we all have this ability to look inwards. That we don't need external forces to tell us we are amazing because deep down, we already know we are.

If nobody else in the world loves you, know that I do. I love your courage, your bravery, your resilience, your heart, your soul, your commitment, and your dedication to live out your best life on this earth. Tell yourself each and everyday that you deserve to be loved, and that you are loved.

Go through life fiercely knowing that you don't need to seek happiness, validations, and approval from others. That you have it inside you all along and that is all you need to keep going.

Chapter 2:
Just Try

Today we're going to talk about a very simple yet important topic. And my goal for this video to see if i can challenge to get you to try something new every day if you feel that your life isn't exciting or have become somewhat stale.

Have you ever come across the saying " you never know until you try"? This explorative mindset has allowed us as children to experience new things, new food, new activities, make you new friends,and to be curious about everything around us. With this curiosity comes a deeper understanding of our likes and dislikes. And we spend more time on the activity that we really and discard those that we don't favour. Some of these likes can turn into solid passions and even careers that we dedicate our lives to, while some other activities we would soon outgrow and move on from.

Regardless of whether we do stick on to these new interests or not is not of importance. What is however, is that we gave ourselves a chance to have a taste of whether something we have not done before could potentially fit into our lives. We gave it an opportunity to be assimilated into our daily routine and activities. And we find new hobbies left and right that make up our identity. Even in school we are encouraged to try new CCAs, new sports, new musical groups to find something we might like besides studying all day to become a more holistic individual. And even in higher education, universities, we are encouraged to explore different subjects if you are in the field of humanities before you settle down on a major that really speaks to you. And many a times we find that we didn't know we liked something until we really gave it a shot.

However as we grow older, which I'm sure many of you experience as well, our sense of curiosity for the things around us starts to diminish with accelerating pace every year. There is no one around us encouraging us to keep up that level of exploration, and when we are left to our own devices, we stop trying new things. We stop looking for things to learn, stop looking for skills to pick up, and we just settle on the things we have already been doing for so long until it bores us to no end. This lack of exploration can seep into our identity, to the point where we stop trying new food, stop finding new friends, or stop putting ourselves in vulnerable positions where we may feel disappointed if things don't work out. We become so cyclical in the way we view life that fear drives us not to venture outside our comfort zone. This fear holds us back from new experiences and we tend to believe at our age of 25 or whatever, that our identity is fixed and that is who we are until the day we die. We stop exploring new job opportunities that are not within our area of expertise, and we stop trying to step out into the unknown for fear of failure.

But if you realize, the great innovators of the world never ceased to try new things no matter at what age they are at. They do not fear the unknown but yet embrace it. Think Steve Jobs, after being ousted Apple, the company he founded, he made Pixar animations into such a remarkable and industry leading animation studio that he came back to Apple and made it one of the most successful companies of all time. He kept trying to make a difference and he tried new opportunities even after the seemingly huge failure of being kicked out of your own company.

Personally, I never stopped trying new things. I am the kind of person that gets bored very easily after working on something for 1 to 2 years, or maybe a maximum of 3 years. When something becomes too simple that it requires no brain power on your part, the task becomes monotonous and robotic. There were many times i felt that there was no purpose in doing such tasks because I wasn't learning anything new. And when I had that mindset of trying something else that might interest me, suddenly that new thing became exciting and I had something to look forward to learning all over again. Even if it meant that it made little to no money as you tried to make an income stream of it at the beginning stages. I was happy nonetheless.

Think back on the times when you genuinely felt good when you tried something new for the first time and it became something you couldn't possibly move forward without. It could be an apple product, and smartphone tablet or headphones, or a job where your creativity is celebrated, or a new sport or hobby that you have no qualms setting aside countless hours in the week to do. These are all products of simply just trying.

Now look back again and think about when was the last time you actually tried something new. If you can't remember when, it was probably too long ago. You may want to consider making trying new things a habit so much so that it just becomes a part of you.

So i challenge each and everyone of you today to say yes to new experiences, things, and people when the next opportunity comes around. You never know what you may be missing out on. And it could potentially be your next passion in life.

Chapter 3:
The Magic of the 5 Minute Rule

Recently I have been struggling to get things done, more so than usual. It has become a daily battle with myself to sit down on my desk to begin the necessary work that I know i need to do. However looking at the endless list of tasks i have in front of me, i can't help but to choose procrastination and slacking over beginning my work. And it has affected my ability to be a productive member of society.

Whilst I knew in the back of my mind that I believe the work that I do can benefit society, and that it has the power to give me freedom of time and money to get and do the things that i really wanted to do in life, on some level it wasn't actually enough to get me to start the work. Many a times I felt really sluggish and it would take some strong reminders to get me motivated enough to start the work. That was the point where i decided i needed to search for a solution that work not only make work more enjoyable, but to also push me to get work started much faster without delay.

After spending some solid hours researching, i came across one strategy that I felt would work like a charm on me. And that is to employ the 5 minute rule to every single task that I have on hand.

The biggest problem that I have currently is that I am working on 10 different projects at any one time. And when I look at these 10 separate projects that need my attention, I can't help but feel overwhelmed about the number of hours that I needed to schedule for each of these projects. And that seemed like a mountainous task for me to climb. And looking at it as a whole, it felt absolutely daunting and impossible. Which was what made me not want to even attempt to begin that climb.

How the 5 minute rule works is that for every project that I needed to work on, I wrote that I only needed to do the task for 5 minutes. However ridiculous that sounded, it actually worked like a charm. My brain was tricked into thinking that this became much more manageable and i would accomplish it easily. And we all know that the biggest problem is getting started. But once u do, you tend to keep going. And so for every task that i told myself i needed to do for 5 minutes, in reality i ended up spending the adequate amount of time i needed to do to get the job done. whether it be 10 minutes, 30minutes, an hour, or even several hours.

I managed to trick my brain into breaking each project down to its most basic manageable form and that gave me to confidence that I could crush it with ease. I applied this technique to not only work, but also going to the gym, walking my dog, and other administrative and personal tasks that I was lazy to do. And i saw my ability to begin each task and eventually check it off my to-do list increase exponentially. My productivity level also skyrocketed as a result.

With this simple trick in your arsenal. I believe anyone that you too can begin your work much quicker as well and crush every single task that will be put in front of you today and in your future. So i challenge each and everyone of you today to just tell yourself that you will only need to set aside 5 mins for each task and see where that takes you, and that I believe will be in the right direction.

Chapter 4:
Meditation The Key To Happiness

Have you ever wondered why people who meditate tend to be the happiest, most grateful and satisfied people on earth? And have you ever wondered why the rest of us always seem to be unhappy about everything that is going on with our lives even though we are incredibly fortunate to be alive?

Many of us have a roof over our heads, smartphones that keeps us connected all the time, friends and family that surround us, but yet we still can't explain why we aren't at peace inside.

We get bogged down by traffic, people around us who seem to rub us the wrong way, and the countless other things that seem to bring us closer and closer to anguish.

Another problem that many of us have to deal with right now is stress. we have deadlines, colleagues, bosses, and paperwork that bring us overwhelm on a daily basis that we find ourselves off balance and in search of our breath.

I want to introduce you to the powerful tool called meditation, and why it is crucial that you employ it in your lives to reduce stress and anxiety and to live a more mindful life starting today.

When we meditate, even to a short 5-10min guided meditation practice that can be found on youtube or even right here on this channel, we bring our awareness to the present moment. And when we breathe and focus on the breath, we allow time for ourselves to be grounded and centered. When thoughts enter our mind, we simply acknowledge them and let them drift on by. This conscious practice of being fully present and deep breathing allows our bodies to relax and destress. And we are much more focused on what we need to do and how we can get to our goals faster.

Through meditation, one can change and rewire our brain to stop thinking of the past and future but to focus on the here and now. With intention, meditation can also help you get what you needed to done faster.

Through my own meditation practice, i have found that it made every day of my life much more purposeful and grounded. Before, i always found myself drifting throughout the day, wasting time, procrastinating, and feeling guilty for not taking action. But with a simple 10min guided meditation practice, i was able to refocus my attention and get my day going as it should without feeling sorry that i had wasted my morning not getting anything done.

Meditation takes time to develop, like a muscle, consistency is the key to success. By devoting 10mins each day to meditation, you are telling yourself that this is the time for yourself, time to reframe all the negative thoughts, to be grateful for your existence, to not dwell on the past, and to focus on the things and people that matter in life. Your body will essentially be "tricked" into automatically feeling abundance, happiness, and joy. The more you do it, the more powerful this technique becomes.

I challenge each and every one of you to try out meditation for yourself, even if i am only able to get through to one person, i am sure you will experience the rich and rewarding experience that meditation can do for you today.

Chapter 5:
How to Learn Faster

Remember the saying, "You are never too old to learn something new"? Believe me, it's not true in any way you understood it.

The most reliable time to learn something new was the time when you were growing up. That was the time when your brain was in its most hyperactive state and could absorb anything you had thrown at it.

You can still learn, but you would have to change your approach to learning.

You won't learn everything, because you don't like everything going on around you. You naturally have an ego to please. So what can you do to boost your learning? Let's simplify the process. When you decide to learn something, take a moment and ask yourself this; "Will this thing make my life better? Will this fulfill my dreams? Will I benefit from it?".

If you can answer all these questions in a positive, you will pounce on the thing and you won't find anyone more motivated than you.

Learning is your brain's capability to process things constructively. If you pick up a career, you won't find it hard to flourish if you are genuinely interested in that particular skill.

Whether it be sports, singing, entrepreneurship, cooking, writing, or anything you want to pursue. Just ask yourself, can you use it to increase your creativity, your passion, your satisfaction. If you can, you will start learning it as if you knew it all along.

Your next step to learning faster would be to improve and excel at what you already have. How can you do that? It's simple yet again!

Ask yourself another question, that; "Why must I do this? Why do I need this?" if you get to answer that, you will find the fastest and effective way to the top yourself without any coaching. Why will this happen on its own? Because now you have found a purpose for your craft and the destination is clear as the bright sun in the sky.

The last but the most important thing to have a head start on your journey of learning is the simplest of them all, but the hardest to opt for. The most important step is to start working towards things.

The flow of learning is from Head to Heart to Hands. You have thought of the things you want to do in your brain. Then you asked your heart if it satisfied you. Now it's time to put your hands to work.

You never learn until you get the chance to experience the world yourself. When you go through a certain event, your brain starts to process the outcomes that could have been, and your heart tells you to give it one more try. Here is the deciding moment. If you listen to your heart right away, you will get on a path of learning that you have never seen before.

What remains now is your will to do what you have decided. And when you get going, you will find the most useful resources immediately. Use your instincts and capitalize your time. Capture every chance with sheer will and belief as if this is your final moment for your dreams to come true.

It doesn't matter if you are not the ace in the pack, it doesn't matter if you are not in your peak physical shape, it doesn't matter if you don't have the money yet. You will someday get all those things only if you had the right skills and the right moment.

For all you know, this moment right now is the most worth it moment. So don't go fishing in other tanks when you have your own aquarium. That aquarium is your body, mind, and soul. All you need is to dive deep with sheer determination and the stars are your limit.

Chapter 6:
Don't Fear Judgement

People often seem to get caught up in certain areas of their lives where they have a lot to offer but don't actually have the guts to be transparent about it. Let me make some sense.

We all have this ability to get distracted by things that have very little to do with our actions. But have a lot to do with what others will say about us.

You go through a rough patch in life and then you find the balance. We have things that have been going on in our lives from the beginning, but we still feel doubts about it.

The doubt is natural. But if the doubts are a result of the presence of other people around you, then you have a problem at your hand. This problem is the fear of judgment that everyone imposes on us in their own unique ways.

Humans have a tendency to get out of their ways and try certain things that aren't always normal. They may be normal for some, but for most people out there, it's just another eccentric doing something strange.

So what? What is so bad about being a little different? What is wrong with thinking a little out of the box? Why should your approach be bad if someone doesn't approve of it?

These questions should not make you feel confused. Rather should help you get a much clearer idea of what you want. These questions and their answers can help you find the right motivation. The motivation to do your thing no matter what the others around you say or see.

You are the best judge of your deeds. Because no one else saw your intentions when you started. No one else saw the circumstances that led you to these actions. No other person was in your head looking at and feeling those incidents that carved your present state. But you were always there and always will be.

No one cares what you are up to until you get to the stage of being noticeable. People pass judgments because now you have made it into some sort of limelight. It may be your workplace, your college, or even a party where most people are stoned.

But think about it, what harm can you get with a couple of remarks about your outfit or an achievement?

The words that strike your ears and make you feel incompetent or stupid are just the insecurities of the people around you. The glare of shaming or mockery is only the reflection of the feeling that they don't have what you have.

So be who you are, and say what you want, and do what you feel. Because the people who mind don't matter. But the people who matter would never mind.

Come to terms with yourself and be confident with what you want to do or are currently up to.

No one would understand your reasons and no one is meant to. But they can make a judgment when you are finally on that rostrum. Then you'd have the power to shut anyone at any time.

Chapter 7:
10 Habits of Meryl Streep

Meryl Streep is an American actress known for her incomparable abilities; she can adapt to complicated accents, sing, be a comedian, and play old male rabbi. Meryl roles have brought her from African bush and Greece beaches, Julia Child's legendary kitchen, and Disney wonderland. If you have watched Meryl ace her roles, this doesn't sound like a standard joke. Meryl is undoubtedly a Hollywood queen with 21 Academy Award nominations and three wins for Kramer vs. Kramer, Sophie's Choice, and The Iron Lady. Rising to such fame, staying modest and brilliant, and, ahem-an an estimation of $ 160 million net-worth, Meryl maintains specific principles.

Here are 10 habits of Meryl Streep to enumerate from.

1. Focus on the Skills Rather Than Looks

During an interview with Vogue, Meryl said that stressing about your weight or skin will derail you. Instead, concentrate on what you enjoy doing, as what you put your hands on should be your world. Meryl had repeatedly reiterated her stance on choosing genius over beauty, even when told she is "too ugly."

2. Focus on the Bigger Picture

It is natural for people to succumb to the muck of stress, deadlines, and anxiety. It is also common to find yourself overcommitting or doubting whether you can do a task or achieve a specific goal. However, if you take a step back and breathe, you will see the bigger picture. Meryl said that the one thing she could tell her 20-something old self would be to think big. She wished she could have devoted more time comprehending the critical role she had in society.

3. Be Authentic

Never, ever apologize for being true to yourself. Meryl was called fat, ugly, and her nose being ridiculed. She recalls how at first, her self-esteem declined to a point she couldn't even watch her shows but later made it her aim to criticize societal expectations of a slim, perfect, and beautiful goddess Hollywood queen.

4. Listen Always

Meryl studies accents as well as what they communicate to stay in tune with the roles she portrays. She achieves this by empathically listening. It means listening before and after work and in between work-to those you associate daily to learn, listening to everything.

5. Age Is Just a Number

Meryl insists on embracing your age and doing what you can utmost at any phase. She has always been vocal against Hollywood manifestations of stripping female actresses short. Meryl has used her influence to fight against ageism, demonstrating that women of all ages deserve to be heard, seen, and appreciated.

6. Start by Starting, Stay Consistent

In the 90s, Meryl kept on making moves despite getting zero Oscar nominations. You have to keep doing what you're doing. Just keep going no matter what.

7. Stay Connected With Your Family

If you are a mother and jogs between 8 to 10 working hours and attending to your family, you hold a soft spot in Meryl's heart. In a podcast, she recounts how her priority was only on those roles that were both location and time-friendly to have quality time with her family.

8. Make the Mold, Then Advance It

After developing an understanding of yourself, set your standards and navigate your way through, which you'll rely on. It is about what feels suitable to you, not what you've been told. Throughout her 45-year career, Meryl has created and reinvented herself, thus ensuring that she improves her talent, craft, and ideas and remaining relevant in Hollywood.

9. Good Things Take Time

In modern society, delayed progress is no progress, and the patient feels worthless than virtuous. Nonetheless, Meryl's career journey is an excellent example of how good things take time because it wasn't until 10 years after acting that she gained the recognition she deserved. Persist at it until you get to where you want to be.

10. Stay Humble

Meryl Streep often referred to as the best actress of her generation, would have within her rights succumbed to the luxuries of being a celebrity. But she chose to stay grounded, and as she told Vogue Magazine that she tried as much to live an ordinary life as when you do your own taming, you cannot get spoilt.

Conclusion

Having has built a successful career from the bottom through her appearances and roles in films and other avenues, Meryl Strip has become an iconic influence that seamlessly defines how you can hit the top by just being you.

Chapter 8:
The Things That Matter

Today we're going to talk about a topic that I am very passionate about. Passionate because it has helped to guide each and every decision that I make on a daily basis. Having this constant reminder of the things that matter will put things in perspective for us - to eliminate the things that are taking up our time for the wrong reasons and to focus on the things that we actually want deep down in our hearts.

With that in mind, let's begin.

How many of you can safely say that you know what truly matters in life? How do you define living a successful and fulfilling life? Is it by having a certain net worth? Is it by living a stress-free life? Is it seeing the world? Is it by serving a defined number of people? Is it by having 10 life-long friends that you can count on? Is it by having a certain number of kids? Or have you not really thought about what you really want out of life yet?

Before we can really gear our actions towards the direction that we want to lead it, we must first know exactly what those specific things we want to achieve are.

The things that matter in my life vary over time as I get older and wiser. When I was young I used to think getting good grades, getting into a good university, and getting a good and stable job was all that really mattered, but I have soon come to realize that family, friends, and having people to hang out with were way more important than simply making money. There was a point in my life that I was so driven by money that I created a huge imbalance in my life by spending 99% of my time on my career. This lopsided drive caused me to neglect friendships, relationships, and soon people associated me with always being too busy for anything. I gradually stopped hanging out with anyone altogether. At first it was okay as I thought "hey, I finally have time to do whatever I want" and I don't have to be disturbed by meetups that would disrupt my workflow. But over time, I felt a gaping hole opening up somewhere deep inside that I could not seem to fill. I suddenly realized that I had successfully isolated myself from any and all relationships. This isolation felt increasingly lonely for me. I felt that I had no one to talk to when I was feeling down, no one to share my struggles with, no one to walk this journey with, and I knew I needed to do something about it. It was only after I started reconnecting with my friends did I truly feel alive again. Having friends brought me more joy than money ever did or could. There's a saying that you can't buy happiness; the same is true for friendships - you can't buy them either. They have to be earned and built with trust and loyalty.

For those of you who are so career focused and money-minded, I share from experience that the destination may not be pretty if you do not have friends or family to share it with. Sure you may afford a penthouse or a Ferrari, but what does it really mean? Sure you have a nice view and a fast ride, but can you share your life with it? When you are old and frail, can your house and car support you physically and emotionally? Don't make the same mistake I did for a good 3 years of my life. It was enough time for me to feel completely alone. No amount of acquiring things could fill that hole no matter how hard I tried. Sure I had the fanciest Apple products, my iPad, iPhone, MacBook, iMac, AirPods, the list goes on. Sure I could "make friends" with these shiny objects by using them everyday. But over time it just reminded me more and more that I had replaced people with gadgets, that I had replaced humans with Siri. It was really really sad honestly.

Having friends that don't judge you or who don't care whether you have money or not, those are the real friends that you know you can count on. And I urge those of you who have neglected this big part to start reconnecting old friends or finding new ones altogether who share the same interests as you. Golf buddies, tennis buddies, karaoke buddies, these are good places to start searching for friends and getting the ice broken.

If starting a family is something that you really want in life, have you begun searching for a partner and planning how and when you expect that to happen for you? Sure many of us think we may have a lot of time to do after we get our career going, but how many of us have heard stories of people who just never got off the bandwagon because they've become too busy with their careers? That maybe getting pregnant just never seems like the right time because you don't want to jeopardize your job. Or maybe that you never even got around to dating at all by the time you are 35 because you've become too busy being a general manager of your company. If having a career is the most important thing to you, then by all means go full steam ahead to achieve that goal. However if family is something of great significance to you, you may want to consider starting that timeline right now instead of waiting. Remember the goal is to focus on the things that truly matter. If having a loving spouse who you can grow old with and having say 2 kids who can support you when you are old is what you really want, maybe waiting isn't such a good idea. Finding love takes practice. You will meet frogs along the way and it takes time to grow a lasting relationship. Sure you can rush a marriage if time is of the essence, but is that ideal? Personally I believe a strong relationship takes 2-3 years to build. Do you have that type of runway to play with? Don't work yourself to death at your job only to find yourself rich and alone. Regret will come after for sure.

Whatever else you have defined as the things that matter to you, make sure that you never neglect those priorities. Sometimes life gets so busy and hectic that we forget to stop and refresh ourselves on what we really want to get out of life. It is all too easy for us to operate on autopilot - To set an alarm, go to work, gym, go home, take dinner, sleep, and repeat the day all over again. For weekends, we may be so exhausted from work that we just end up sleeping or wasting our weekend away only to begin the same routine again on Monday.

There's plenty of time for work decades down the road, but dating relationships and friendships may not have that runway of time.

So I challenge each and everyone of you to clearly define what the things that matter mean to you and to take consistent action in these areas day in and out until you can safely say you've already checked them off your bucket list.

Chapter 9:

<u>Stop Ignoring Your Health</u>

Do you have a busy life? Do you follow a hard and continuous regime of tasks every day for a significant amount of time? Have you ever felt that you cannot enjoy even the happiest moments of your life even if you want to? Let me highlight one reason you might recognize it straight away. You are not enjoying your days while still being in all your senses because you don't have your mind and body in the right place.

All these years you have lived your life as a race. You have taken part in every event in and around your life just because you never wanted to miss anything. But in this process, you never lived your life to its full potential. You never lived a single moment with just the emotional intention of being then and there and not trying to live it like just another day or event.

People often get so busy with making their careers that they don't realize what is more important in life? It is their mental and physical health!

You will not get anywhere far in your life if you keep ignoring the signs of sickness your body keeps giving you. Your body is a machine with a conditional warranty. The day you violate the conditions of this warranty, life will become challenging and you won't even be interested in the basic tasks at hand.

You might have heard the famous saying that "Health is Wealth". Let it sink in for a while and analyze your own life. You don't need to be a top-tier athlete to have a good body. You need a good body for your organs to work properly. You need an active lifestyle to be more productive and be more present and engaged in the things that are going around you.

The dilemma of our lives is that we don't care about what we have right now, but we care a lot about what we want. Not realizing that what we want might be cursed but what we have is the soul of good living. And that my friends are the blessing of health that most of us take for granted.

Most people have a tendency and devotion to work specifically on their health and fitness on a priority basis. They have a better standard of life. These people have a clearer mind to feel and capture the best moments in life with what their senses can offer best to them.

If you don't stop ignoring your health, you won't ever get out of this constant struggle. The struggle to find the reasons for you being detached from everything despite being involved every time.

Being careful and observant of your health doesn't make you selfish. This makes you a much more caring person because not only your life but the life of others around you is also affected by your sickness. Not only your resources are used for your treatments but the attention and emotions of your loved ones are also being spent, just in hope of your wellness.

Chapter 10:
How To Not Live Your Life In Regret

Today we're going to talk about a simple yet profound topic that I hope will awaken something in you today if you have been sleeping on the wheel of your life. I hope that with this video, I can help you to stop wasting precious time and to keep doing the things that you've always said you wanted to do right now this day. Not tomorrow, but today.

Before we go any further, I want you to write down the things you wish to accomplish before you die. It can be as small as saying I love you to your mom and dad, to something bigger like quitting your job to find something you are passionate about, to leisurely things such as travelling to XXX countries by whatever age. To things such as picking up an instrument that you've always wanted to learn but told yourself you just didn't have the time or that you wont be able to do it, or other things such as making new friends, starting a family, or literally anything under the sun.

I want you to write these things down no matter how big or small, and make them a bucket list of sorts. Many people think that a bucket list is always a leisure thing, but many a times, our bucket list could be more significant in that it is something that we don't just want to do, but need to do.

We may not fill every single thing on that bucket list, but if we can even do half of them, we can say that at least we have tried and we don't regret a single thing. The fact that we attempted is sometimes good enough, it is definitely better than not even trying and living with the guilt of "what if".

Now that we have got this list down. I'm going to jump right into the one thing that will help us put all of this into perspective. And help us truly see what matters at the top of our list. And I think you will be surprised that it may not have anything to do with travel and leisure, but it is the personal goals that we have been putting off.

Are you ready for it?

I want you to close your eyes right now. Find a quiet space where no one will disturb you for the next 5-10mins. I want you to pause this video if you need to at any one point. And I want you to visualise yourself at your deathbed, at the end of your life, whether you see yourself being 80, 90, 100, or even 60 or 70, if you feel that maybe u dont see yourself living a long life. Whatever it may be, I want you to picture yourself in your last moments.

Now I want you to ask yourself, what do you regret not having done in your 20s, 30s, and 40s. What is that one thing that you just couldn't live with yourself having not done, and what that greatest regret may be. Was it not committing your life to helping others, was it not pursuing your passion? Was it not being a good father, mother, child, friend, lover?

What is it? Who do you see around you? Are there any friends that are there to see you off? Are there any family members, cousins, loved ones there? Or have you not been a good person that none of them are there to see you? Are you lonely or surrounded my love? Are you happy that you've kept your word and done the things you said you would? Or do you regret not trying?

Do you feel like your heart is full because you have conquered every experience that life has to offer? Or do you regret not spending enough time outside seeing the world for what it truly is? Do you regret not moving to a country that you said you would one day, and just lived to see people live their best lives vicariously through Instagram and Facebook and YouTube? I want you to be as honest as you can with yourself about your current actions and project them forward into the future. Are they going to bring about the kind of peace that you would feel at the end of your life knowing you've done everything you possibly can and without regret?

Take some time to think about the things I said and see if you can paint a vivid picture of what they is like. Did you commit to eating healthily that you can see yourself living to a ripe old age? Or are you consuming junk food everyday that you can't even realistically see yourself being healthy past the age of 50?

As you are visualising these, I want you to write down any thoughts that passed through your head as you see these images. Are there any new priorities that you didn't know existed? Any shift in your bucket list?

Anything that jumped out to the front of the queue that you need to fix right this second? or to start doing right now?

If you are done I want you to open your eyes. How did that feel? Was it a surreal feeling to imagine yourself dying and looking back on your life, your teens, your 20s, your 30s. What were your biggest regrets and biggest accomplishments?

I want you to take this bucket list with you and take action on them. If you can prioritise them according to practicality, do it. If there are some easy tasks that you want to execute in next 6months, I want you to start them now. If your goal is to make some new friends that you can take to your golden years, I want you to start searching for them now so that you don't end up old and alone. Being lonely is one of the worst things that can happen to you, and I dont wish that on anyone. If you need to build up some friendships, dont waste time, because friendships takes time to nurture, and you don't want to end up in a situation that you don't have anyone to look for support, comfort, and simple companionship as you grow old.

I challenge each and everyone of you to live your life to the fullest, to live a life without regret, and that starts by taking action on the things that matters the most. It is not always about becoming a millionaire or a billionaire, because money can't buy everything. Money can't buy friends, it can't buy companionship, and it will not last. Build and create things that you can take with you right up to your death bed. And Remind yourself that life is short and not worth wasting.

Today we're going to talk about a topic that hopefully helps you become more aware of who you are as a person. And why do you exist right here and right now on this Earth. Because if we don't know who we are, if we don't understand ourselves, then how can we expect to other stand and relate to others? And why we even matter?

How many of you think that you can describe yourself accurately? If someone were to ask you exactly who you are, what would you say? Most of us would say we are Teachers, doctors, lawyers, etc. We would associate our lives with our profession.

But is that really what we are really all about?

Today I want to ask you not what you do, and not let your career define you, but rather what makes you feel truly alive and connected with the world? What is it about your profession that made you want to dedicated your life and time to it? Is there something about the job that makes you want to get up everyday and show up for the work, or is it merely to collect the paycheck at the end of the month?

I believe that that there is something in each and everyone of us that makes us who we are, and keeps us truly alive and full. For those that dedicate their lives to be Teachers, maybe they see themselves as an educator, a role model, a person who is in charge of helping a kid grow up, a nurturer, a parental figure. For Doctors, maybe they see themselves as healers, as someone who feels passionate about bringing life to someone. Whatever it may be, there is more to them than their careers.

For me, I see myself as a future caregiver, and to enrich the lives of my family members. That is something that I feel is one of my purpose in life. That I was born, not to provide for my family monetary per se, but to provide the care and support for them in their old age. That is one of my primary objectives. Otherwise, I see and understand myself as a person who loves to share knowledge with others, as I am doing right now. I love to help others in some way of form, either to inspire them, to lift their spirits, or to just be there for them when they need a crying shoulder. I love to help others fulfill their greatest potential, and it fills my heart with joy knowing that someone has benefitted from my advice. From what I have to say. And that what i have to say actually does hold some merit, some substance, and it is helping the lives of someone out there.. to help them make better decisions, and to help the, realise that life is truly wonderful. That is who i am.

Whenever I try to do something outside of that sphere, when what I do does not help someone in some way or another, I feel a sense of dread. I feel that what I do becomes misaligned with my calling, and I drag my feet each day to get those tasks done. That is something that I have realized about myself. And it might be happening to you too.

If u do not know exactly who you are and why you are here on this Earth, i highly encourage you to take the time to go on a self-discovery journey, however long it may take, to figure that out. Only when you know exactly who you are, can you start doing the work that aligns with ur purpose and calling. I don't meant this is in a religious way, but i believe that each and every one of us are here for a reason, whether it may to serve others, to help your fellow human beings, or to share your talents with the world, we should all be doing something with our lives that is at least close to that, if not exactly that.

So I challenge each and everyone of you to take this seriously because I believe you will be much happier for it. Start aligning your work with your purpose and you will find that life is truly worth living.

Chapter 11:
Blaming Others In Your Life For Your Mistakes

When something goes wrong, are you more likely to own up to the mistakes you made, or play the blame game?

Many people are quick to point fingers and play the blame game. In fact, recent research has shown that we *expect* this behavior to happen. We expect to experience others engaging in blame-shifting, placing the blame on others for their own mistakes.

My hands aren't clean. I've blamed people for my own mistakes more than once, that's for sure. Why? It's easy.

Simply put, it's much easier to place the blame on someone else than to take full responsibility for your actions. It's also easier to blame someone for our actions rather than take a deeper look at why we made the mistake that we did and face possible consequences — whether it was something you did at work or something that happened during a tiff between you and your partner. Blame shifting takes less effort, and it's easier on us emotionally — at least in the moment.

"Blame is like another defense mechanism,". "We could call it denial or projection, because it helps us preserve our sense of self-esteem or pride by avoiding awareness of our own issues."

Why do we use defense mechanisms? To protect ourselves — whether it's from criticism, negative consequences, attention, whatever it is you're afraid of. You might even be in denial that you are, in fact, the one who's making mistakes.

"We can think of it as a tool we use when we're in attack mode,". Alternatively, she notes that some people blame others in an attempt to hurt them — which is certainly not cool!

Furthermore, it's possible that you might have some deep rooted negative experiences from your childhood that make you predisposed to acting in this way. "Psychologically, we can also see that attachment issues can create problems that manifest when we grow up,". "Insecure and ambivalent attachments can lead to us not accepting responsibilities and finding blaming easier."

Seldom does blaming others for our mistakes come without consequences. It might feel like we're winning in the moment, benefitting ourselves when we don't take responsibility for our actions, but that's definitely not the case in the long run. Blaming others can, and likely will, backfire on you, leaving you wishing you never played the blame game in the first place.

If it wasn't obvious, those you blame *will* realize it, and they're not going to be happy that you're not owning up to your own blunders. As with many toxic behaviors, acknowledging that you have the problem is the first step to addressing it. Even acknowledging it might not be easy for you, since finally, you'll have to take the blame yourself, and hold yourself accountable for your actions. If you're a chronic blamer, it might have been a while since you took responsibility for yourself.

We have to learn to be able to hold ourselves accountable for mistakes big and small, even though it can be scary. It's not easy to own up to our errors, but without a doubt, it's the right thing to do.

Chapter 12:

How to Love Yourself First

It's so easy to tell someone "Love yourself" and much more difficult to describe *how* to do it. Learn and practice these six steps to gradually start loving yourself more every day:

Step 1: Be willing to feel pain and take responsibility for your feelings.

Step 1 is mindfully following your breath to become present in your body and embrace all of your feelings. It's about moving toward your feelings rather than running away from them with various forms of self-abandonment, such as staying focused in your head, judging yourself, turning to addictions to numb out, etc. All feelings are informational.

Step 2: Move into the intent to learn.

Commit to learning about your emotions, even the ones that may be causing you pain, so that you can move into taking loving action.

Step 3: Learn about your false beliefs.

Step 3 is a deep and compassionate process of exploration—learning about your beliefs and behavior and what is happening with a person or situation that may be causing your pain. Ask your feeling self, your inner child: "What am I thinking or doing that's causing the painful feelings of anxiety, depression, guilt, shame, jealousy, anger, loneliness, or emptiness?" Allow the answer to come from inside, from your intuition and feelings.

Once you understand what you're thinking or doing that's causing these feelings, ask your ego about the fears and false beliefs leading to the self-abandoning thoughts and actions.

Step 4: Start a dialogue with your higher self.

It's not as hard to connect with your higher guidance as you may think. The key is to be open to learning about loving yourself. The answers may come immediately or over time. They may come in words or images or dreams. When your heart is open to learning, the answers will come.

Step 5: Take loving action.

Sometimes people think of "loving myself" as a feeling to be conjured up. A good way to look at loving yourself is by emphasizing the action: "What can I *do* to love myself?" rather than "How can I *feel* love for myself?"

By this point, you've already opened up to your pain, moved into learning, started a dialogue with your feelings, and tapped into your spiritual guidance. Step 5 involves taking one of the loving actions you identified in Step 4. However small they may seem at first, over time, these actions add up.

Step 6: Evaluate your action and begin again as needed.

Once you take the loving action, check in to see if your pain, anger, and shame are getting healed. If not, you go back through the steps until you discover the truth and loving actions that bring you peace, joy, and a deep sense of intrinsic worth.

Over time, you will discover that loving yourself improves everything in your life—your relationships, health and well-being, ability to manifest your dreams, and self-esteem. Loving and connecting with yourself is the key to loving and connecting with others and creating loving relationships. Loving yourself is the key to creating a passionate, fulfilled, and joyful life.

Chapter 13:
Start Working On Your Dreams Today

When did you get up today? What was your day like? What did you achieve today? Did any of that matter?

Maybe it didn't because you don't have any dreams to work towards, or maybe that you've forgotten what they are altogether.

To have a dream is to have a direction in life. To have a dream means you have something bigger than yourself that you want to achieve.

Everyone gets at least one chance in their life to actually go and pursue that dream, but few recognize that until it is too late. It is too late to regret when you are on your deathbed wondering what could have been. That is when it is too late to work on your dreams. When you have no more time left.

The Moment to start working On your dreams is right here right now.

We repeat our failures every day but never learn. We get depressed every day but never communicate. We get bullied every day, but never fight back. Why?

Is it because we can't do it? No, Definitely Not! We can do it whenever we want. We can do it today. We can do it the next minute. We just lack Ambition!

Every day someone achieves something big. Some more than often, others maybe not their whole life. But the outcome is **not** determined by **fate**, but with **Effort**.

All the billionaires you see today started out with a few dollars just like you and me. They just had the guts to pursue their dream no matter what the cost is. They all had a vision of something bigger. They went full throttle even when everyone around them expected them to fail. Even when they met with struggles that hit them harder than the last, they were still focused on the dream. Never did they once lesson the effort.

No two persons are born the same. Not the same face, color, intelligence, or fate. But what's common for every human being is the built-in trait to strive for a goal once they are determined enough. Doesn't matter if it's food for the next meal or success for the times to come.

The struggle is real, it always was, it always will be. The world wouldn't be what it is today if it weren't for the struggle man has gone through over the centuries. The struggle is the most real definition of life in this world. But that doesn't mean it's a bad one.

Our parents struggled to make us a better person. They put in their best effort to watch us succeed in our dreams. Their parents did the same for them and their parents before them.

This is what makes life a cycle of inherited struggle and hardships. Nobody asks to struggle through a hard life, but we can all turn the hard life into a meaningful one. The life that we all should expect to eventually achieve only if we keep the cycle running and if we keep putting in the effort.

How then do we actually work towards our dreams? By focusing on the things that matter each and every day, again and again, until that mountain has been conquered. Don't forget to enjoy the journey, because it could well be the best part of the trip up top.

You never know what the next moment has in it for you. You can never predict the future, but you can always hope for a better one. You only get the right to hope if you did what was meant to be done today. It's your lawful right to reap the fruit if you took care of sowing the seeds faithfully and diligently all through the year.

The motivation behind this continuous grind of time in search of that Dream lies in your past. You cannot achieve those dreams until you start treasuring the lessons of your past and become a person who is always willing to go beyond.

You can't simply depend on hope to get something done. You have to reach the point where start obsessing over that goal, that thing, that DREAM. When you start obsessing, you start working, you start seeing the possibilities and you just keep going. If you don't get up then you WILL miss the moment. The moment that could have made all the difference in the world. If you don't act upon that impulse, you might never get that inspiration ever again. And that will be the moment you will always regret for the rest of your life.

Remember that your whole life is built on millions of tiny decisions. A decision to just act on one of those moments can transform your life completely. These moments often test you too. But only for an inch more before you find eternal glory. So don't wait for someone else to do it for you. Get up, buckle up, and start doing. Because only you Can!

Chapter 14:
How To Take Action

Today we're going to talk about something pretty crucial. And this also plays into the topics of motivation, purpose, and goals. And that is, "How To Take Action". Before we begin, i want you to write down a couple of things that you were supposed to take action on but have been putting it off for whatever reason. And i want you to keep these things in mind as we go through this video. And hopefully by the end of it, i would have been able to convince you to take action and to start moving forward in your bigger life projects as well.

Why is Taking Action so important? To put it simply, taking action is the one thing that we can control to move us towards our goals. Whether we succeed or not is irrelevant in this case. Many of us hesitate to take action because we are afraid of failure. We fear the unknown and we over analyse and over think things to a point that we become paralysed. And I'm sure you guys have heard this term before: and that is analysis paralysis.

We draw up such detailed plans for how to are going to tackle this problem, we tweak and tweak the draft, aiming to find perfection before we even take the first action step to begin doing the work. And many times, for many people, we just let the plan sit on the shelves or in our computer, afraid to take action because we fear that we might not be able to accomplish the goal we have set out for ourselves.

You see, planning and drafting isn't going to move the needle. When we have a project, planning only makes up a small part of the process. And completion of the project is always down to every member of the group taking action and completing their part of the task. Or in the case of a solo project, all of the action and effort put in comes from you.

When we plan for anything, even for our future, it is something that keeps us in check, to have a reference for us to know that we are on the right track. But whether or not we follow those plans are entirely up to the actions that we actually take. Whether we do save that $100 every month, or not spend money on unnecessary things, or say that we are going to invest in constant education and growth, these are not set in stone if we do not take action.

Another thing that holds us back from taking action is the fear that we will make mistakes. And that we will feel like a fool if we did things wrongly. But if you look at your life, realistically, how many times have you actually done something right the first time around on something that you haven't actually tried before? For example riding a bike, swimming, learning a new language, learning a new instrument. Wouldn't you agree that making mistakes is actually part of the process? Without practice there's not perfect, so why do we think that we will always get it right the first time when it comes to starting a new business or taking action on whatever new thing that we had set our sights on?

We have no problem telling ourselves that making mistakes in smaller things is okay but we berate ourselves or we create this immense expectation that we must get things right the first time around on bigger projects that we fear the climb because we fear the thought of falling down. And we don't even give ourselves a chance to prove that we can do it.

To counter this, we must tell ourselves that making mistakes is a part of the process, to not rush the process, and to give ourselves more room for failure so that we will have the best chance of actually succeeding someday. However long it takes. We must trust the process because it will happen for us eventually. The only time we really do fail is the last time we actually stop trying, stop taking action, and stop learning from our mistakes. that is the time when we can say we are a failure, if we quit. But if we never give up, and we keep taking action, it will work out for us.

One final hurdle that many of us face is that we tend to want to rush the process and we set unrealistic deadlines to achieve those goals. If we go back to our previous example of learning a new instrument, how many of you guys will agree that, although not impossible, it is unrealistic to become a guitar guru after the 1st year? Most of us would realistically say that it will take at least a few years of daily practice to actually become a pro guitar player. But how many of us actually apply that same concept to a big project like growing our income from $3k to $10k. We all expect fast results and fast growth, but rarely does things work out so smoothly, unless we are incredibly lucky.

When we set these big targets but fail to realise that we need to take baby steps consistently everyday, we set ourselves up for failure without realising it. Without giving ourselves the room to grow a seed into a tree, we end up chopping it down when it is still at the early growth stages. And we fail to let time and effort do it's thing, giving it water and light day in and day out. And we beat ourselves up when we quit prematurely.

What I have learnt, from experience, is that the best way to achieve something eventually, is to take baby steps, taking a little action each day, be it 5 mins, an hour, or 10 hours, they all count. And instead of just hoping to rush to the end, that I actually learned to not only enjoy the process, but also to trust that my efforts will all pay off in the end. And many a times, they did. I left the fear and worry to one side and just focused on taking action. I stopped comparing myself with my peers, and focused on my own journey. I can't control how much faster my competition can grow or achieve, but i can definitely control my own destiny.

So i challenge each and everyone of you today to take a look at the list of things that you hope to achieve that you have written down at the start of this video, and to take the first step of stop trying to perfect the plan, to stop thinking and worrying about what might and could go wrong, to stop fearing the unknown, and to simply just take a little action each day. The worse thing that you can do to yourself is to not even try. You will make mistakes along the way, but as long as you learn from them, you will be moving in the right direction.

Chapter 15:
Live Life To The Fullest

Have you ever felt like others don't understand your pain when they seem to be living a happy life? You're not alone in feeling this way, but the truth is that happiness takes work, and learning how to live life to the fullest takes dedication and practice.

People who smile in public have been through every bit as much as people who cry, frown, and scream. They just simply found the courage and strength to smile through it and enjoy life in the best way possible.

Life is short, and we only live once. Learning to live life to the fullest is an important step in making the most of every day.

Whether it's taking care of your children, working hard on your career, writing a new blog post each day, or baking up fabulous creations, you get to decide how you enjoy spending your time. Your parents, friends, community, and society in general all have their opinions, but at the end of the day, you're the only person who will be around for every moment of your life.

Do what makes you happy, and everything else will fall into place. This may not mean finding your perfect job if you're limited by education, location, or job openings. However, you can still do what you love by engaging in hobbies, volunteer work, or mentoring.

Sometimes there's danger involved in life, but every reward carries risk with it. If you never take risks, you'll never get anywhere in life, and you certainly won't learn how to live life to the fullest.

Staying in your comfort zone is the fastest way to become discontent Without stepping outside what you're already comfortable with, you will cease to learn and stagnate in both your personal and professional life. While it may feel uncomfortable, taking a risk can be as simple as saying yes next time your friends want to go out instead of staying at home alone. It can mean going out on a blind date, buying plane tickets to a new city, or dragging out those paints that have been stuffed away for years.

When people look back on their lives, <u>they regret the chances they didn't take</u> more than the ones they did, so find something new to try today and set goals beyond what you currently believe possible.

You'll hear people say, "I had that idea," every time you see someone create something great. Everyone had the idea for Facebook first. The reason Mark Zuckerberg got rich off of it is because he went out and did it while everyone else was talking about it. Learning to live life to the fullest is a big step in discovering a path that will lead you to your greatest sense of happiness and accomplishment. We all need moments to rest and relish in a sense of contentment, but staying in one place too long will leave you feeling a lack in life. Discover what makes your life feel meaningful and go after it.

Chapter 16:

Removing The Things In Your Day That Don't Serve A Purpose for You

Today I went to a yoga class and felt that something was not quite right. I did not enjoy it as much as I used to. As I was acting out the poses that the teacher was instructing to us, i found myself wondering what the heck I was doing on my yoga mat. Something i used to look forward everyday suddenly became a chore to me, and I didn't understand why.

I had been forcing myself for the past month thinking that I needed the class to stretch and to feel more flexible. But the more i attended, the unhappier I was. And it was only after I decided to completely remove yoga from my itinerary did I feel my day was actually more enjoyable.

Many times we plan things in our day just for the sake of it. We plan things because we think we have to, even if it didn't bring much joy into our lives.

I would like you to think of some of the things in your week, what are those that don't bring joy to you? Could you replace them with something that you might find a little more enjoyable instead?

i believe that many of us try to pack so much into our schedule thinking that the busier we are, the more meaningful our lives are, the more we are getting out of it. While it might be true to a certain extent, over doing and over subscribing can actually be counter-productive for us. All of us need rest and relaxation to recharge and tackle the next day. If we are packing our schedule of things we hate, we will never truly be at peace in life. It is okay to stop the things that stop bringing you joy, and maybe coming back to it at a later time.

I found myself loving to spend time stretching by myself while listening to music rather than doing it in a yoga class. And as soon as I replaced this block of time with something that I enjoyed, it made my day that much better, even if it was just a little.

Start taking a hard look at everything we are putting our time, energy, and commitment to, what are the areas that we should trim that don't serve us anymore, and how can we either replace them with something better or just freeing up time to rest and sleep instead until we figure it out.

You may find yourself just a little bit happier.

Chapter 17:

How To Achieve Peak Performance In Your Career

What exactly do we mean by peak performance? Well, it is defined as the state when you are at your best, delivering the results and feeling in the flow. You're able to overcome the challenges and feel at ease about your work and life. Getting in a state of peak performance at work is all about being motivated, managing your energy, staying productive, and developing the proper habits. We have a finite supply of energy that we expend throughout the day, but we aren't taught how to cultivate this energy. The ultimate key to higher performance is learning how to manage your energy all through the day consciously. The challenge is, once you have reached your peak performance, you have to stay and perform in that state as constantly as possible; you have to sustain the level of peak performance. Here are some ways for you to achieve peak performance in your career.

1. **Being Motivated About The Work**

The best way to stay motivated I to choose something that you're both good at and love to do. Work on something that keeps you energized and motivated. When you do this type of work, you're more likely to operate in a flow state and achieve peak performance. But, as much as we like, there won't always be things that favor our interest. In those situations, it's helpful to reframe the problem that fits the "why" purpose. For example, if you are unwilling to do something, but there's an urgency, and you're bound to do it, you will find a way and energy to get with it anyway. It would be best to start focusing on the gains and benefits you will get from doing the things you dislike. This will keep you somewhat motivated to do it. Or you can ask for help from someone who loves doing the work that you hate. It's all about reframing the situations to your best interest.

2. Developing The Right Habits

Achieving peak performance is more about the actions you take and the thoughts you think. Having negative thoughts like "will I be able to do it?" or "what if he/she is better at it than me?" and so forth will only make you anxious. It will be like driving with the handbrake on, and your performance will only be a drag. Instead, try and develop positive thoughts. Get on with the attitude of "I can do it" or "I can learn from my colleagues if I mess up." Adopting such positive thoughts will give you a huge boost towards your peak performance. Behavior habits can also hurt your performance just as severely. For example, if you have a habit of arriving late, start getting ready 10-20 minutes earlier than you usually do. If you are afraid to speak up, try saying anything for the first 60 seconds, so your voice is at least heard.

3. Staying Productive

Alongside having the motivation and the right habits, try to get more work done with the same or fewer resources; whether it's time, money, energy, you'll be steps ahead. Being productive also means that you can create extra time for the next task, thinking, or simply to recharge.

Banishing obstacles like procrastination and perfectionism can help you achieve your peak performance. Address the things that are holding you back. Assess and evaluate them, stay on track by planning your day the night before.

4. Managing Your Energy

You can generate more and more of your energy, that's the best thing about it. It is a renewable resource, while time is not. Therefore, it is essential to manage your energy and protect your time. One way you can manage your energy is by matching your tasks with the day that best suits you. If you are more productive and creative in the morning, start doing the more significant and more critical tasks in that time, and leave the small ones for later. The prominent energy creators revolve around your health and wellness, both physical and mental. Get a good night's sleep every day, have a proper diet, and exercise regularly.

5. Be Consistent

The single most important thing you can do for your career is to show up every day. No skill or talent can beat the power of consistency. Being consistent will continue to maximize your potential for peak performance and give you an upper hand over those who tend to take the opposite of consistency. As you continue to learn and apply the new lessons you have learned from your experience at work, your ability to perform at peak will stay on the upward side of the scale longer than expected.

Conclusion

Above everything else, we should remember that sustaining peak performance at work doesn't have to be your hit or miss gamble. You should know your numbers and plot out strategies for compounding improvements and set measurable goals to work. This will give you not only a progressive routine but also some direction and clarity. Embrace the momentum turn to stay in the flow state longer than your co-workers or the last time you did. Track your performance and continue to beat your current record to keep yourself motivated and full of confidence.

Chapter 18:

6 Ways To Define What Is Important In Your Life

In this crazy world that we live in, the course of evolution spirals upward and downward, and the collective humanity has witnessed glorious times and horrific ones. The events around us change minute-to-minute. So much seems out of our control, but we find solace in knowing that one thing remains within our immediate control; taking back ownership and responsibility for ourselves. If life has gotten away from you and you feel overwhelmed, anxious or depressed, then maybe it's time to stop and refocus on what's most important to you and find a way back to what really matters to you.

The idea is to evaluate what you're actually doing with and for yourself, determine if it's even essential to you, and then make the said necessary changes that will best accommodate your needs, interests, and desires. Here are some ways to consider how and on what things you should refocus your attention to determine what is most important in your life.

1. **Determine What Things You Value Most**

Choose and focus on the things around which you have to structure the life that you want to create. When you consciously make these choices, you are more focused on reminding yourself what things in your life you can't and won't do without. These all represent the backbone of your life. We often forget that people and events play a massive role in shaping up to our lives. They Mold us into what we have become so far and what we are to become in the future. Their support and encouragement in our lives are undeniable. We have to see which people and what events we value the most in our lives and then should keep our focus on them more.

2. Decide What Commitments Are Essential To You

Keeping the above valuable things in mind, evaluate which commitments do you value the most in your life. Commitments are the obligations you enter into willingly and represent your promise to see any relationship/project/contract conclusion steadfastly. Renegotiate your essential commitments, if necessary, but consider completing the existing commitments that you are already obligated to and refuse to take any new ones if you aren't ready. That way, you will focus more and fulfill those commitments first that are more significant to you and your life.

3. Assess The Way You Use Your Time

Most of us have a fixed daily routine, with many fixed activities, habits, and chores. Evaluate which things are absolutely necessary and vital for shaping up your life and yourself daily. Assess the time you spend communicating, how much of your time you spend online, emailing, texting, or on your cell phone. How can you cut back the amount of time spent on these activities to do something more productive? How much time are you spending on TV, radio, reading newspapers and magazines? Consider decreasing your consumption and receive the basic information from a reputable source only once throughout the day. Avoid repetition and redundancy.

4. Get Rid of Any clutter That's In Your Life

Look around you and see, do you need everything you have? Give away anything that you haven't used since the last two years. It could be anything, from selling items to furniture, clothing, shoes, etc. Anything that you no longer need. Someone else can happily use what you haven't all this time. And not just the worldly things; get rid of all the emotional and psychological clutter you have kept aside for so long, and it no longer serves you. We have to get rid of the old things to make room for the new things to come. This will help us reflect on our actual being of who we are and where we are.

5. Spend More Time With People That Matter To You

Evaluate how much quality time you actually spend with your family and close friends. As life evolves, more people will enter into your sphere. These people may fall into different categories of importance in your life, such as acquaintances, colleagues, friends, partners, etc. Our time is precious, so it is wise to use it on those that matter to us the most. It's necessary to sort out our interactions and to assess the meaning of each relationship to us.

6. Make Time To Be Alone

It all comes down to how much time do you make yourself at the end of the day? What was the last time you spent doing something you're passionate about or what you love doing? Give yourself all the time and permission to express your creativity and make peace with your mind. Take care of your body, spirit, and mind because these are the things that will make you feel alive. Take a walk and look around, reacquaint yourself with all the beauty around you. Make each breath count.

Conclusion

Identifying and understanding your values is a challenging but as well as an essential exercise. Your personal values are a central part of defining who you are and who you want to be. By becoming more aware of these significant factors in your life, you can use them as your best guide in any situation. It's comforting and helpful to rely on your values since most of our life's decisions are based on them.

Chapter 19:

Five Habits For An Extremely Productive Day

Our productivity and efficiency during the day are variables of several factors. Some days seem better, the sun a little brighter than normal; the food tastes sweeter and the mood lighter. In such days, unmatched joy bubbles within us increasing our productivity exponentially. Many people cannot choose when to experience these days. Instead, they are at the mercy of their emotions and the influence of other people who can ruin their day whenever they please.

Here are five habits for an extremely productive day:

1. Plan For Your Day Beforehand.

Failure to plan is planning to fail. A plan is an integral part of success. It means that you understand the obligation you have to live the day ahead and the duties and responsibilities in your in-tray. A plan will help you check all the boxes on your to-do list and you can track your progress in each.

In planning for your day, you will know the resources that you have and those that you lack. It is also possible to budget on your means earlier rather than waiting for the actual day and start scampering for resources. A wise man does not live on a borrowed budget but within his own.

A good plan is a job half done. Your day will be more productive when nothing takes you by surprise because you would have anticipated every occurrence beforehand and it will find you armed with a solution.

2. <u>Wake Up Early</u>

The early bird catches the worm. Punctuality is very important if you want to have a productive day. An early riser has a fresh and clear mind compared to those who wake up late and start their routine fast because they are behind schedule. They do not have the advantage of calmness and composure because they want to make up for time lost. This exposes them to error and ridicule from their enemies if they fail, which is imminent because of their inaccuracy.

When one wakes up early, one has an advantage over other people. They can open their businesses or start their work earlier than their competitors do. They maximize their productivity because they have created enough time for each task they had scheduled. Consider waking up early to have an extremely productive day.

3. <u>Do Not Bite More Than You Can Chew</u>

This calls for sobriety in the handling of tasks and designing of goals. The pressure to outdo yourself can be overwhelming enough to make you lose focus on what is at stake. It is paramount to set realistic and achievable goals so that you can concentrate on them. Shun anything that presents itself to you that is beyond your ability no matter how attractive it seems.

The power of self-control is at play. Resist the temptation of going out of your way to prove a point for the sake of it. Instead, fully concentrate on what you had planned. Schedule anything outside your plan to the following day. It is far from procrastination because in this case, you have a clearly defined timeline on when to actualize your plans.

Failure to develop this habit will lead you to a situation where you have many unfinished tasks. This is not productivity, by all standards. Focus on what you can manage and do it efficiently.

4. <u>Avoid Negative Company</u>

A negative company will derail your progress and work. When you associate yourself with such people, you will not see the unseen benefit in challenges and instead, you will focus on the undone, incomplete, and failed bits of your work. Failure is contagious. If you constantly surround yourself with a clique of failures, you too shall fail.

To have a productive day, have friends who share your vision. You will blossom under their shade and they will encourage you in your work. This will show you possibility even when you see failure and doom. In their company, your days will be productive and joyful.

5. <u>Look At The Bigger Picture</u>

As you seek to have productive days, look at the bigger picture. It will make you focus on the greater plan you have rather than petty squabbles and meaningless distractions that come your way. The bigger picture will always remind you of your cause and inspire you to live up to it even when challenges come your way.

When you pay attention to the above five habits, you will have extremely productive days. It all lies in your effort to adopt them.

Chapter 20:

How Your Beliefs And Moods Contribute To What's Going On In Your Life

Because our ability to successfully interact with other people is so important to our survival, these skills have become part of human nature. We determine whether to help in large part on the basis of how other people make us feel, and how we think we will feel if we help or do not help them.

Positive Moods Increase, Helping

I do not need to tell you that people help more when they are in good mood. We ask our parents to use their car, and we ask our boss for a raise, when we think they are in a positive mood rather than a negative one. Positive moods have been shown to increase many types of helping behavior, including contributing to charity, donating blood, and helping coworkers (isen, 1999). It is also relatively easy to put people in a good mood. You might not be surprised to hear that people are more likely to help after they've done well on a test or just received a big bonus in their paycheck. But research has found that even more trivial things, such as finding a coin in a phone booth, listening to a comedy recording, having someone smile at you, or even smelling the pleasant scent of perfume is enough to put people in a good mood and to cause them to be helpful (baron & thomley, 1994; gueguen & de gail, 2003; isen & levin, 1972).

In another study, van baaren, holland, kawakami, and van knippenberg (2004) had students interact with an experimenter who either mimicked them by subtly copying their behaviors outside of their awareness or did not mimic them. The researchers found that people who had been mimicked were more likely to help, by picking up pens that had fallen on the floor and by donating to a charity. It is quite possible that this effect is due to the influence of positive moods on helping—we like people we see as similar to us and that puts us in a good mood, making us more likely to help. In sum, the influence of mood on helping is substantial (carlson, charlin, & miller, 1988), so if you're looking for help, ask on a nice day, subtly mimic the person's behaviors, or prepare some good jokes.

But why does being in a good mood make us helpful? There are probably several reasons. For one, a positive mood indicates that the environment is not dangerous and therefore that we can safely help others. Second, we like other people more when we are in good moods, and that may lead us to help them. Finally, and perhaps most important, is the possibility the helping makes us feel good about ourselves, thereby maintaining our positive mood. In fact, people who are in good moods are particularly likely to help when the help that they are going to give seems likely to maintain their positive mood. But if they think that the helping is going spoil their good mood, even people in good moods are likely to refuse to help (erber & markunas, 2006).

In the end, we cannot completely rule out the possibility that people help in large part for selfish reasons. But does it really matter? If we give money to the needy because we will feel bad about ourselves if we do not, or if we give money to the needy because we want them to feel good, we have nevertheless made the contribution in both cases.

Chapter 21:
Making Sky The Limit

Your attitude determines everything, whether it's in your personal life or your professional one. You ask any millionaire or billionaire how they got on top of their game and how they got to where they are, and they will undoubtedly tell you that they mastered their mind before mastering their game of success. So, the question arises, what exactly do we need to do to get to the next level? Some people strive for bigger things and achieve their goals against all odds, and they are not at all constrained by conventional thinking. Irrespective of their area of interest and chosen fields, they have certain experiences and characteristics in common. We now look at some of the things that we need to maintain to have a sky's-the-limit mindset.

Mastering your mind for the sky's-the-limit mindset comes up with the most crucial key, accepting rejection. We all have faced and experienced rejection at some point in our lives. But if we let it consume us and allow it to fester, it can lie dormant and negatively affect our lives. There are a million examples in front of us who faced rejections but are now extremely successful. Take J.K. Rowling; she was a single mother living on welfare and struggling to support her child. She faced repeated rejections but never gave up. Her first Harry Potter book got sold for about €4000. Now she's even richer than the Queen of England.

We all want to be successful, but are we ready to put in the blood, sweat, and tears it takes to get there? Thinking big and doing big takes willpower and a lot of work, the amount of work that isn't a piece of cake for everyone. Malcolm Gladwell tells us that if you want to be an expert or champion in something, you must be willing to devote 10,000 hours to it (90 minutes a day for 20 years). And if you're doing so, you need to feel passionate about it too. Van Gogh sold only one piece during his lifetime, but his passion drove him to paint almost 900 works.

Understand that we are flawed creatures, and we are bound to make mistakes. Bill Gates may be the world's richest man, but even he says that his failures served him as a great learning tool. Thomas Edison took between 1,000 to 10,000 tries before creating the world-changing invention. See your failures as a part of your journey. Without them, you won't be able to succeed much. And if they can fail, what makes you think you can't?

Be confident in your abilities and trust yourself. Surround yourself with good people who will help you accomplish things. People who would clap at your success and help you during your failures. Welcome every opportunity with open arms. Find the good in every situation, no matter how bad it looks on the outside. Every experience has its value, identify and cherish those experiences that serve you with opportunities to learn. The only thing stopping you from being successful is yourself.

Chapter 22:
Five Habits of A Healthy Lifestyle

A healthy lifestyle is everybody's dream. The young and old, rich and poor, weak and strong, and male and female all want a happily ever after and many years full of life. The price to pay to achieve this dream is what distinguishes all these classes of people. What are you ready to forego as the opportunity cost to have a healthy lifestyle?

Here are five habits for a healthy lifestyle.

1. **Eating Healthy Food**

Your health is heavily dependent on your diet. You have heard that what goes inside a man does not defile him, but what goes out of him does. In this case, the opposite is true. What a man takes as food or beverage affects him directly. It can alter the body's metabolism and introduce toxins in the body hence endangering his life.

Most people do not take care of what they feed on. They eat anything edible that is readily available without any consideration. All other factors like the nutritive value of the food and its hygiene are secondary to most modern people who have thrown caution to the wind. Towns and cities are full of fast food joints and attract masses from all over. It is the most lucrative business these days. Are these fast foods healthy?

As much as the hygiene could be up to standards (due to the measures put in place by authorities), the composition of these foods (mostly chips and broiler chicken) is wanting. The cooking oil used is full of cholesterol that is a major cause of cardiac diseases. To lead a healthy lifestyle, eating healthy food should be a priority.

2. Regular Exercising

The human body requires regular exercise to be fit. Running, walking, swimming, or going to the gym are a few of the many ways that people can exercise. It is a call to get out of your comfort zone to ward off some lifestyle diseases. It is often misconstrued that exercising is a reserve for sportsmen and women. This fallacy has taken root in the minds of many people.

Unlearn the myths about exercises that have made most people shun them. The benefits of exercising are uncountable. It improves pressure and blood circulation in the body. Exercises also burn excess calories in tissues that would otherwise clog blood vessels and pose a health hazard. Research has shown that most people who exercise are healthy and fall sick less often. This is everyone's dream but the few who choose to pay the price enjoy it. Choose to be healthy by doing away with frequent motor vehicle transport and instead walk. A simple walk is an exercise already. When you fail to exercise early enough, you will be a frequent patient at the hospital. Prevention is always better than cure.

In the words of world marathon champion, Eliud Kipchoge, a running nation is a healthy nation.

3. Regular Medical Checkup

When was the last time you went for a medical checkup even when you were not sick? If the answer is negative or a long time ago, then a healthy lifestyle is still unreachable. A medical examination will reveal any disease in its early stages.

In most third-world countries, healthcare systems are not fully developed. Its citizens only go to the hospital when a disease has progressed and is in its late stages. At such a time, there is a higher probability of the patient succumbing to it. Doctors advise people to seek medical attention at the slightest symptom to treat and manage long-term illnesses. Regular medical checkups help one become more productive at work.

Is a healthy lifestyle attainable? Yes, it is when one takes the necessary measures to fight diseases. Regular medical checkups can be financially draining. Seek an insurance policy that can underwrite your health risks and this will make medical expenses affordable.

4. Staying Positive

A bad attitude is like a flat tire. If you do not change it, you will never go anywhere. There is a hidden power in having a positive attitude towards life. It all starts in the mind. When you conceive the right attitude towards life, you have won half the battle.

A healthy lifestyle starts with the mind. If you believe it, you can achieve it. So limitless is the human mind that it strongly influences the direction of a person's life. As much as there are challenges in life, do not allow them to conquer your mind or take over your spirit. Once they do, you will be constantly waging a losing battle. Is that what we want?

Associate with positive like-minded people and you will be miles away from depression and low self-esteem. We all desire that healthy lifestyle.

5. Have A Confidant And A Best Friend

Who is a best friend? He/she is someone you can trust to share your joy and sadness, and your high and low moments. You should be careful in your selection of a confidant because it may have strong ramifications if the friendship is not genuine.

A confidant is someone you can confide in comfortably without fear of him/her leaking your secrets. He/she will help you overcome some difficult situations in life. We all need a shoulder to lean on in our darkest times and a voice to comfort us that it is darkest before dawn. This helps fortify our mental health. We grow better and stronger in this healthy lifestyle.

These are the five habits for a healthy lifestyle. When we live by them, success becomes our portion.

Chapter 23:
Bounce Back From Failure

Failure is a big word. It is a negative word most say. It is cursed in most cases. It is frowned upon when it is on your plate. But why?

Sure, it certainly doesn't feel good when you encounter failure. We can't even forgive ourselves for failing at a simple card game. We get impatient, we get hopeless and ultimately we get depressed on even the smallest of failure we go through in everyday life.

Why is it that way? Why can't we try to change a failure into something better? Why can't we just leave that failure right there and not try to make a big deal out of each and every small little setback?

These questions have a very deep meaning and a very important place in everyone's life.

Let's start with the simplest step to make it easy for yourself to deal with a certain failure. Whenever you fail at anything, just pause for a second and talk to yourself.

Rewind what you just went through. Talk to yourself through the present circumstances. Think about what you could have done to improve at what you just did. Think about what you could have done to prevent whatever tragic incident you went through. Or what you could have done to do better at what you felt like failing at.

These questions will immediately sketch a scenario in front of your eyes. A scenario where you can actually see yourself flourishing and doing your best against all odds.

Whatever happened to you, I am sure you didn't deserve it. But so what if you

Lost some money or a loved one or your pet? Ask yourself this, is it the end of the world? Have you stopped breathing? Have you no reason left to keep living?

You had, you have, and you will always have a new thing, a new person a new place to start with. Life has endless possibilities for you to find. But you just have to bounce back from whatever setback you think you cannot get out of.

Take for example the biggest tech billionaires in the world. I am giving this example because people tend to relate more to these examples these days. Elon Musk started his carrier with a small office with his brother and they both lived in the same office for a whole year. They couldn't even afford a small place for themselves to rent.

There was a time when Elon had to decide to split his last set of investments between two companies. If he had invested in one, the other would have gone down for sure, just to give a chance to the other company to maybe become their one big hit. Guess what, he ended up keeping them both because he invested in both.

Why did he succeed? Was it because he wasn't afraid? No!

He succeeded because he had Faith after all the failures he had faced. He knew that if he kept trying against all odds and even the obvious risks, he will ultimately succeed at something for what he worked so hard for all this time!

Chapter 24:
How to Value Being Alone

Some people are naturally happy alone. But for others, being solo is a challenge. If you fall into the latter group, there are ways to become more comfortable with being alone (yes, even if you're a hardcore extrovert).

Regardless of how you feel about being alone, building a good relationship with yourself is a worthy investment. After all, you *do* spend quite a bit of time with yourself, so you might as well learn to enjoy it.

Being alone isn't the same as being lonely.

Before getting into the different ways to find happiness in being alone, it's important to untangle these two concepts: being alone and being lonely. While there's some overlap between them, they're completely different concepts. Maybe you're a person who basks in solitude. You're not antisocial, friendless, or loveless. You're just quite content with alone time. You look forward to it. That's simply being alone, not being lonely.

On the other hand, maybe you're surrounded by family and friends but not relating beyond a surface level, which has you feeling empty and disconnected. Or maybe being alone just leaves you sad and longing for company. That's loneliness.

Short-term tips to get you started

These tips are aimed at helping you get the ball rolling. They might not transform your life overnight, but they can help you get more comfortable with being alone.

Some of them may be exactly what you needed to hear. Others may not make sense to you. Use them as stepping-stones. Add to them and shape them along the way to suit your lifestyle and personality.

1. Avoid comparing yourself to others.

This is easier said than done, but try to avoid comparing your social life to anyone else's. It's not the number of friends you have or the frequency of your social outings that matters. It's what works for you.

Remember, you have no way of knowing if someone with many friends and a stuffed social calendar is happy.

2. Take a step back from social media.

Social media isn't inherently bad or problematic, but if scrolling through your feeds makes you feel left out and stresses, take a few steps back. That feed doesn't tell the whole story. Not by a long shot.

You have no idea if those people are truly happy or just giving the impression that they are. Either way, it's no reflection on you. So, take a <u>deep breath</u> and put it in perspective.

Perform a test run and ban yourself from social media for 48 hours. If that makes a difference, try giving yourself a daily limit of 10 to 15 minutes and stick to it.

Don't be afraid to ask for help.

Sometimes, all the self-care, exercise, and gratitude lists in the world aren't enough to shake feelings of sadness or loneliness.

Consider reaching out to a therapist if:

- You're overly stressed and finding it difficult to cope.
- You have symptoms of anxiety.
- You have symptoms of depression.

You don't have to wait for a crisis point to get into therapy. Simply wanting to get better and spending time alone is a perfectly good reason to make an appointment.

Chapter 25:
Happy People Stay Present

"Realize deeply that the present moment is all you ever have."

According to a study, 50% of the time, we are not fully present in the moment. We are either thinking about the past or worrying about the future. These things lead to frustration, anxiety, and pain in our daily life. Each morning as soon as we wake up, we start seeking distractions. As we wake up with a clear mind, we should be grateful for a new day that we got; instead, we start looking for our phone, start going through interwebs and rush into our days. So now we are going to help you and list some of the things that will help you stay present.

Stop Being a Slave to Your Mind: For the next four days, let's do an exercise where you pay attention to your thoughts and see what crosses your mind. You. You will soon realize that majority of the thoughts that you have are destructive. There will be very little time to think about the present, and the majority of your thoughts would be about the past or the future. So, whenever this happens and you find yourself wandering consciously, try to bring yourself back to the present. Also, you need to remind yourself that multi-tasking is a myth and focus on one thing only.

Tap into Your Senses: If you mindfully tap into your senses, you will realize that it is a fantastic way of bringing more awareness into your day. Because our eyes are wide open all day, we can see, but we forget to tap into other senses such as taste, touch, or smell. But if you use these, you can feel more present and calm down if you are in a stressful situation. You might not realize this, but our senses play a huge role in manifesting our reality. For example, everything we are hearing we are touching will regularly turn into our reality. That is why we can use the power our senses have and feel more calm and present.

Listen Closely: Everyone loves to talk, but only a few people like to listen. People love to share their dreams, what they have accomplished and what they desire, and still, nobody seems to be listening closely.

"When you talk, you are only repeating what you already know. But if you listen, you may learn something new."

When you listen carefully, you will be able to charm people and at the same time learn new things and be present. Because you will be focusing on what they are saying, you will focus on the current moment. This way, you will also be able to silence your thoughts about the past and future because you will be consciously listening and focusing on what they are saying. This will also benefit your relationship in the long run because when you need an ear to listen to your problems, they will be there for you. This is a win-win situation for you, and you will improve your relationship while practising being more present.

Chapter 26:

5 Lessons on Being Wrong

Being wrong isn't as bad as we make it out to be. I have made many mistakes, and I have discovered five major lessons from my experiences.

1. Choices that seem poor in hindsight are an indication of growth, not self-worth or intelligence. When you look back on your choices from a year ago, you should always hope to find a few decisions that seem stupid now because that means you are growing. If you only live in the safety zone where you know you can't mess up, then you'll never unleash your true potential. If you know enough about something to make the optimal decision on the first try, then you're not challenging yourself.

2. Given that your first choice is likely to be wrong, the best thing you can do is get started. The faster you learn from being wrong, the sooner you can discover what is right. Complex situations like relationships or entrepreneurship have to start before you feel ready because no one can be truly ready. The best way to learn is to start practicing.

3. Break down topics that are too big to master into smaller tasks that can be mastered. I can't look at any business and tell you what to do. Entrepreneurship is too big of a topic. But, I can look at any website and tell you how to optimize it for building an email list because that topic is small enough for me to develop some level of expertise. If you want to get better at making accurate first choices, then play in a smaller arena. As Niels Bohr, the Nobel Prize-winning physicist, famously said, "An expert is a person who has made all the mistakes that can be made in a very narrow field."

4. The time to trust your gut is when you have the knowledge or experience to back it up. You can trust yourself to make sharp decisions in areas where you already have proven expertise. For everything else, the only way to discover what works is to adopt a philosophy of experimentation.

5. The fact that failure will happen is not an excuse for expecting to fail. There is no reason to be depressed or give up simply because you will make a few wrong choices. Even more crucial, you must try your best every time because the effort and the practice drive the learning process. They are essential, even if you fail. Realize that no single choice is destined to fail, but that occasional failure is <u>the cost you must pay if you want to be right</u>. Expect to win and play like it from the outset.

Your first choice is rarely the optimal choice. Make it now, <u>stop judging yourself</u>, and start growing.

Chapter 27:
How To live Your Best Life

This is a simple yet not easy topic to tackle. But I am sure that this question is something that all of you are aspiring to achieve in life. Because really, being on earth, being alive, it does not have any real significance if we do not live it to our fullest potential, to enjoy every single wonderful thing that life has to offer, to smell the flowers, to see the sights along the way, and to appreciate the little things while going for the big dreams.

For many of us, I do believe that it was a lot easier to live our best life while we were in school. Whilst the pressure of school and getting good grades were always constantly hanging over us, that was the case for every other kid around us. It was fair game. And we all strived to be the best student that we could possibly be. At the same time we had time to pursue our interests, learn new things, learn new skills, and even new instruments. The possibilities were endless and the world was our oyster. We explored the deepest oceans and in my opinion, we were indeed living our best lives as children and teens.

Making friends and hanging out with them frequently either through study or play weren't difficult. We were social creatures and we were really good at that.

However as we grew older, into our twenties and beyond, we start to lose that spark. That wonder. That curiosity. That vision that the world was in the palm of our hands. Instead, that view became more myopic, it keeps shrinking, work gets in the way, and we lose our sense of wonder and curiosity. We become more cynical and dull. And we stopped really trying to live our best life.

The introvert in us starts to come out more and more, and we retreat into our homes watching Netflix and YouTube, rather than going out there into the world and doing something significant or fun. In today's topic we are not going to talk about careers or income, because i do not believe that you need to be incredibly successful monetarily to be described as living your best life. But rather it's the other things that make up who you are that matters here.

And for many of us, it has become all too easy to retreat into the comfort of our home after a long day's work and decide that it is perfectly good to just lay on our couches and do nothing all day or weekend. We gradually disconnect ourselves from the outside world and we live in our own little bubble. And we think it is okay.

However what we fail to realize is that over time, these hours add up to days, weeks, months, and even years. And we realise that at the end of it all, we have nothing to show for it. We have not put ourselves in positions where we are exposed to new experiences and things. Of fostering meaningful friendships that would last u to till the end of your life. And we find ourselves alone and regretting that we had not utilised our time more wisely to build up those relationships or creating those experiences that we can look back on and say I'm glad i did all those things. I'm glad i left no stone unturned. I'm glad i did not waste my time doing nothing.

So to sum it all up, i believe that to live your best life, we should all look back at our middle school and high school days. What were we doing then that made everything so interesting and exciting, and how can we integrate more of that into our lives instead of choosing isolation. Whether that be trying out a new activity, learning a new sport, or even simply just hanging out with friends that you can rely on on a much more regular basis. I do believe that you will start to feel that life has much more meaning and happiness will soon follow.

Chapter 28:
How To Set Smart Goals

Setting your goals can be a tough choice. It's all about putting your priorities in such a way that you know what comes first for you. It's imperative to be goal-oriented to set positive goals for your present and future. You should be aware of your criteria for setting your goals. Make sure your plan is attainable in a proper time frame to get a good set of goals to be achieved in your time. You would need hard work and a good mindset for setting goals. Few components can help a person reach their destination. Control what you choose because it will eternally impact your life.

To set a goal to your priority, you need to know what exactly you want. In other words, be specific. Be specific in what matters to you and your goal. Make sure that you know your fair share of details about your idea, and then start working on it once you have set your mind to it. Get a clear vision of what your goal is. Get a clear idea of your objective. It is essential to give a specification to your plan to set it according to your needs.

Make sure you measure your goals. As in, calculate the profit or loss. Measure the risks you are taking and the benefits you can gain from them. In simple words, you need to quantify your goals to know what order to set them into. It makes you visualize the amount of time it will take or the energy to reach the finish line. That way, you can calculate your goals and their details. You need to set your mind on the positive technical growth of your goal. That is an essential step to take to put yourself to the next goal as soon as possible.

If you get your hopes high from the start, it may be possible that you will meet with disappointment along the way. So, it would be best if you made sure that your goals are realistic and achievable. Make sure your goal is within reach. That is the reality check you need to force in your mind that is your goal even attainable? Just make sure it is, and everything will go as planned. It doesn't mean to set small goals. There is a difference between big goals and unrealistic goals. Make sure to limit your romantic goals, or else you will never be satisfied with your achievement.

Be very serious when setting your goals, especially if they are long-term goals. They can impact your life in one way or another. It depends on you how you take it. Make sure your goals are relevant. So, that you can gain real benefit from your goals. Have your fair share of profits from your hard work and make it count. Always remember why the goal matters to you. Once you get the fundamental idea of why you need this goal to be achieved, you can look onto a bigger picture in the frame. If it doesn't feel relevant, then there is no reason for you to continue working for. Leave it as it is if it doesn't give you what you applied for because it will only drain your energy and won't give you a satisfactory outcome.

Time is an essential thing to keep in focus when working toward your goals. You don't want to keep working on one thing for too long or too short. So, keep a deadline. Keep a limit on when to work on your goal. If it's worth it, give it your good timer, but if not, then don't even waste a second on it. They are just some factors to set your goals for a better future. These visionary goals will help you get through most of the achievements you want to get done with.

Chapter 29:
10 Habits of Mariah Carey

Mariah Carey has earned not only a "diva" reputation but also a legendary pop icon for over 30 years in the spotlight. She's an American singer-songwriter, actress, and record producer who has lauded her as a "songbird supreme" and the "queen of Christmas." Despite a challenging start, her debut album charted no. 1 in the US, went multi-platinum, and earned her Grammy Awards for Best Female Vocalist and Best Artist.

She is one of the most successful female performers of all time, with more than 200 million albums sales landing her a net worth of $320 million. Her distinctive acute euphonies and melismatic runs continues shaping pop music up to date. If you're wondering how this simple New York girl climbed up to becoming this legendary, this is for you!

Here are the ten habits of Mariah Carey.

1. Made the Most of What She Was Good At

According to Mariah Carey, she discovered her singing strengths at the age of 6 when her friend, whom she was singing with while holding hands, surprisingly stopped to listen to her. It was from this moment she realized that she had something exceptional and devoted to it. Knowing your strength and devoting entirely to it will eventually land you a lucky spot.

2. Leave No Doubt

Taking your game to the next level can be daunting, and it takes confidence to do so. Mariah Carey's career began magically, but it wasn't long before trolls and haters sprouted. Trolls accused her of being "studio warm" because her voice was so flawless, to be true. She was so troubled by such critics that she decided to shock her detractors with a live performance on MTV.

3. Passion Never Goes Wrong

When Mariah decided to ditch her pop image to focus on R&B and Hip Hop, her decision, as she mentioned in an interview, did not sit well with her record label at first. But eventually resulted to a breakthrough album that is still regarded as the best to date. That's what happens when you believe in your abilities and take a stand for them. Simply put, you're the one who knows how far your abilities can stretch.

4. Forget Plan B, Go Hard on Plan A

To meet your success, you need one well-thought-out plan. With a well-organized plan, make decisions that are in line with your ultimate success objectives. Mariah Carey's music was her life and she was serious and ambitious. Go all in and carry out your only plan as if your life depended on it.

5. Persistence

Perseverance, not talent, is the secret to success. "I knew in my heart that one day I'd make it... Every day that I made it through, I knew I was getting closer to my goal. "Every night, I would thank God for the day when I didn't give up or be knocked down," Carey said in an interview. When you are ambitious, pushing hard is core to achieving your goals.

6. She's All About Equality

If you have a platform, use it to propel influence against societal injustices. Carey received the GLAAD Ally Award in 2016 for her support of the LGBT community. She once assisted one of her backup dancers in proposing to his boyfriend on stage. According to GLAAD CEO Sarah Kate, Mariah Carey has always inspired and encouraged numerous LGBT admirers worldwide with her unwavering commitment to acceptance and inclusive campaigns.

7. A Little Downtime Won't Harm

Mariah mentioned her prior husband's mental and emotional abuse, as well as the chaotic filming of Glitter, in an interview. She worked 22 hours a day, which harmed her mental health and led to her hospitalization in 2001. Your lofty goals demand a healthy mind and body.

8. Explore Constantly

Allow yourself to make mistakes and explore without feeling obligated to deliver a saleable piece every time. Because of Mariah's daring explorations, Male-female collaborative raps and melodies were created by hip hop artists. There's a lot more, but the bottom takeaway is that Maria Carey's daring approach to music paid off.

9. Dream Big

You don't need to know how you'll accomplish the tremendous success you want for yourself; all you need to know is that it will happen. Carey envisioned herself taking off the music industry without doubt and also surpassing Joan Crawford's manor's splendour.

10. Follow Your Superiors

If opportunities don't come knocking at your door, make a door. When Mariah first started recording demos in high school, she met older and more experienced musicians than her. And boy, did she learn! It's also where she worked with Brenda K. Starr, a Puerto Rican freestyle singer. It was through the star that she got noticed by big bosses.

Conclusion

Of course, you don't need to follow suit completely, but you can learn from the divas herself that faith, desire, perseverance, and how serious you take your dreams important manifestation tools.

Chapter 30:
10 Habits of Jennifer Lawrence

Jennifer Lawrence is one of Hollywood's most famous actress, thanks to her role in films such as "The Hunger Games" and "Silver Linings Playbook." But, before her tremendous success, Lawrence struggled to build a name for herself as an actress and model in New York, where she moved when she was 14 years old. After breaking out as the tough-as-nails teenager Ree in the 2010 indie drama "Winter's Bone," Lawrence went on to star in multiple "X-Men" films and drama such as "American Hustle."

I can't think of anyone who doesn't adore Jennifer Lawrence. What is it about this actress that makes her so appealing? It's easy to list a thousand reasons to admire Jennifer Lawrence -from her incredible skill to her quick-witted humour- but honestly, the life lessons she attracts everyone to her.

Here are 10 life habits that Lawrence offers as lessons simply by being herself.

1. Strive for Health and Strength

"I'm never going to starve myself for a part," she declared on the cover of Elle in December 2012. "I don't want little girls to think, 'Oh, I want to look like Katniss; hence I'll skip meals." When you're trying to get your physique to appear just suitable, Emma on the other end is trying to make her body appear muscular and robust rather than skinny.

2. Refresh Yourself

How many times has Lawrence stumbled? That's what probably comes to your mind every time you see her trip over the hem of her gown at an awards presentation. Can anyone blame the girl for this? Those outfits appear to be impossible to walk in! But she trips, and every time, without fail, she gets back up and continues walking.

3. Accept Responsibility for Your Mistakes

Lawrence's awkward moments are all the more endearing because she is always the first to laugh at how clumsy she is when she stands. Remember when she collapsed at the 2013 Academy Awards? Or when she collapsed on the red carpet of the 2014 Academy Awards? What does it matter? We're all human, and J. Law never tries to hide it by acting cool and so should you.

4. The Truth Will Set You Free

Even if your truth seems to hurt more, such as that you pee very quickly or that your breasts are unequal, J. Law says that it is what it is, and to be anything other than herself isn't allowed. Embrace your flaws!

5. Look Past the Hype

Remember to key in what's genuine and what's not, and to keep your things in perspective, look past those who take themselves too seriously.

6. Maintain An Open Mind

Lawrence told E! News that her acting job will not bind her for the rest of her life. However, she understands that things happen and that people's lives change, and she is prepared to keep an open mind about it. Being open-minded will direct you to break the monotony for future possibilities.

7. Nobody Is Flawless

Can you recall a scene in American Hustle in which Lawrence's character discusses nail polish? Do you remember the nail polish? She claims it's the smell that keeps drawing her back since it's delicious on the outside but rotten on the inside. Not only is it a beautiful moment, but the discussion is a metaphor for everyone's good and evil sides. Nobody is flawless, and no one loves it when others claim to be.

8. Humility

During a BBC Radio 1 interview, Lawrence remarked her involvement in "The Hunger Games," where she genuinely adores watching the movies she makes because she gets to see how much of a troll, bad, and untalented is. Weird! Indeed, you wouldn't agree with her right? Bu she's adorable because she is humble.

9. Maintain a Sense of Humour

During an interview with Vogue, Lawrence sense of humour could be seen when she cracked a joke on how seeing 13-year olds give her nightmares. She effortlessly doesn't take life too seriously.

10. Love Your Body

Lawrence has spoken out numerous times about her body, challenging unrealistic beauty standards. She claimed in an interview with FLARE magazine that she would rather appear overweight on camera (and appear normal) than diet only to dress like a scarecrow. That is a whole lot of body positivity just for you!

Conclusion

Jennifer will teach you profound truths- when she acts, and when she put on a mask that conceals who she truly is. She given up none of her power by leaving the covers on the screen and refusing to act to "fit in" with Hollywood culture.

Chapter 31:
10 Habits of Kamala Harris

Kamala Harris smashed the world's record by being the first Black-Asian Woman Vice President of the United States and has held high-level roles early in her career. Her career kicked off as a lawyer and quickly rose to prominence for high-profile handling cases. Her efforts could later land her the position of the district attorney, which elevated her to new heights when she was elected as California Attorney General, and US Senator.

With her empathetic, communicative, and leadership style, Kamala Harris exudes an executive presence that makes her an outstanding leader. Moreover, seeing her in a high position, addressing the nation, conveys that women can achieve everything they set their minds to.

Here are 10 Kamala Harris habits that are worth mentioning.

1. Gender Isn't a Limit.

Kamala is an inspiration to women's success in male-dominated fields. Gender, according to her, should not limit you from pursuing your dreams just because they are stereotypically not for you. She believes that both men and women should have equal access to resources for achieving greatness.

2. Make Informed Decisions

The choices you make today will have a significant impact on your future. According to Harris, tackle everything with due diligence. Having served in the public service for many years, she understands the importance of making informed choices or decisions.

3. Family Comes First

Some Professions demand huge sacrifices, which is why you should have your family closer for a shoulder to lean on. Kamala believes that if it were not for her family's help, she would not have excelled both as a lawyer and a politician. Remember that while others might leave your side during challenging times, your loved ones will never.

4. Don't Sit Around and Complain, Do Something!

Let's face it, it's either you choose to take action or continue complaining about things and not bother. During the Wilmington protest, Kamala thanked her mother for these wise words; "don't sit around and complain, do something." Every day she allows her mother's sentiments to inspire her daily tasks, which is why she is always winning.

5. Nothing can be more delightful than a smart joke.

Kamala's knack for humor helped her in winning hearts. Remember how she reacted to Donald Trump Jr.'s tweet mocking her laugh? The former president mocked her laugh and jokes as long and lame. Her response was just delightful, "You wouldn't know a joke if one raised you."

6. Her Executive Presence

Communicating as a leader is much more than what you say; it also includes your ability to dominate a room and make your presence known. Assessing how Harris makes a speech or speaks during an interview reveals that she effortlessly communicates with authority and elegance. She is not hesitant to allow her personality and femininity to shine through. Her vibrant personality, general friendliness, and captivating grin make her appear very approachable and trustworthy.

7. Connect Ambition With Purpose

As she stated in her memoir "The Truths We Hold: An American Journey," Harris's only goal was to be the solution, which saw her participating in bill formulation and change activism throughout her career. Although she got ridiculed following her rose to prominence, Harris is an example of why you should clarify your ambitions to drive you through your purpose.

8. Have a Voice To Stand for Your Values

There is no doubt that the US can feel Kamala's striking voice. She has been both an active writer and public speaker, even criticizing Trump's administration's failure to handle COVID-19 accordingly. She told the "New York Times" that when you're in a room with everyone expecting you to use your voice with pride and in a way that represents them, you realize how powerful your voice can be.

9. Flaunt Your Achievements

Harris introduced herself during the "Virtual Democratic National Convention" via her prosecutorial stories to familiarize herself with voters, highlighting her accomplishments in fighting gang and gang-related violence, sexual assault, and other issues. Women have been humbled as a result of patriarchy's consequences in order not to offend others. Like Harris, a little hot air is required to rise to get the job or any other role.

10. Show Your Vulnerability

As a leader, expressing vulnerability shows that you are also human. It also shows that you can relate to those listening to you. Harris does not shy off –of who she is and the challenges she faces.

Conclusion

Like Harris has demonstrated, be a leader that speaks up, chooses changes, stands your ground, and always acts with grace.

Chapter 32:
10 Habits of Lady Gaga

Stefani Joanne Angelina Germanotta, the one-and-only Lady Gaga is known for her unique approach to music and life. The iconic American singer, songwriter, and actress has captivated audiences with her talent and kindness, her creative stage appearances, and her dedicated support of the LGBT community and anti-bullying campaigns.

Like many other great success stories, her path to fame was fraught with hiccups, including dropping out of school, being dropped by Def Jam, and eventually writing for Sony. This encounter introduced her to Akon, who assisted her in signing a deal and releasing her first album. Her career has yielded several Guinness World Records, twelve Grammy awards, an Oscar, a BAFTA award, two Golden Globes, and numerous other honors.

Here are 10 Habits of Lady Gaga.

1. She's Inspired by What's Next

Focusing on the present and future makes you the happiest and successful person. During an interview with Oprah, Gaga shared, "I know it's there, but can I open it?" It's not only writing one song; it's also writing the next. It's writing the next chapter of whichever lobe in my brain is still locked."

2. Lady Gaga Owns Fame

Faking it till you make it is a part of almost everyone's game for attention and legacy building. Although it may necessitate a bit of bravado, it puts in a happy outlook and a great groove. If you don't like this phrase, consider Gaga's fine art of manifestation, she saw herself as a success story which eventually laid a ground for her career.

3. Be unique

Lady Gaga is unmistakable in her uniqueness. She distinguishes herself from many female pop artists by her physical appearances, acting, performances, song-writing, and her unique electric genre. You have to be one-of-a-kind, unusual, and shine in your way.

4. Create an Experience To Tell Your Story

Lady Gaga knows how to create a game-changing experience that truly embodies who she is and what she wants to communicate. Think of 2011 Grammy Awards when she was carried down the red carpet in an egg by staffers dressed in a suggestive egg-shell lie outfit? Whatever you are communicating will be memorable, when you relay it through experiences.

5. Don't Conform to Others' Opinions

Everyone will have an opinion on everything, and if you let them, they may influence how you see yourself. Or how you go about your daily existence. For Gaga, getting advice is not something she takes lightly;

instead, she vets whoever offers it. "Only respect those whose opinions you appreciate." she told CNN.

6. Reinvent When Something Isn't Working

Find new ways to getting things done when it's not working anymore. Lady Gaga has dabbled in acting gigs (American Horror Story and A Star Is Born), all while expanding her fan base and showing her diverse talents.

7. Her Art Is Her Solace

During an interview with Rolling Stone, Gaga compared her music with addiction to heroin, suggesting that music is her solace. When you love what you do, no matter the industry, you commit yourself to the struggle and pain that comes with it. It is through ups and downs that you can appreciate your process.

8. Creativity and Hard Work Fuel Her Day-And Her Life

Although singing and writing are natural talents, Gaga is quick to warn aspiring musicians and performers that hard work and sacrifice counts. Gaga believes that learning and mastering your craft should let the you shine through, regardless of the critics. She understands that grit will be the secret ingredient that gets you there.

9. Lead With Values

Gaga constantly advocates for people in society who are ostracized and bullied because they are different such as LGBT. When you identify yourself with beliefs or things that connect with other people, you'll definitely earn their loyalty.

10. She Stays True to Her Personality

Being a leader in your craft entails keeping true to yourself rather than being a follower. If you work as a janitor, be a visionary janitor who instills wonder in your work. Lady Gaga does not behave in a way that is meant to please the public. She forges her way through her outlandish clothes and great performances. Then there's the lead.

Conclusion

It doesn't matter if you have fans, customers, clients, employees, or Gaga's "little monsters." This is how it works, even if you weren't born with the same genes as Lady Gaga. When we push the envelope and step outside of your comfort zone, amazing things happen. Rock your way through!

www.ingramcontent.com/pod-product-compliance
Lightning Source LLC
Chambersburg PA
CBHW072205100526
44589CB00015B/2377